LEARN
YOUR
LINES

LEARN YOUR LINES

WHAT TO SAY WHEN CLIENTS PUT YOU ON THE SPOT

JONATHAN STARK

To Erica, Cooper, and Maggie

YOUR FREE BOOK IS WAITING

PIGEONHOLE YOURSELF

TRANSFORM YOUR POSITIONING FROM SOGGY TO SOLID WITH 21 REAL-WORLD EXAMPLES

JONATHAN STARK

LOOKING FOR MORE?

You might enjoy a free copy of my book on how to make your business more memorable, attractive, and unique in the minds of your ideal clients.

Pigeonhole Yourself:
Transform Your Positioning From Soggy To Solid With 21 Real-World Examples.

Inside, you'll learn:

- The #1 thing you must do before engaging in marketing of any kind
- How to get word of mouth referrals without even asking
- The one thing to say when someone asks, "So... what do you do?"
- The 4 components of a laser-focused positioning statement
- The secret to differentiating yourself from your competition
- and more...

Click the button below for your free copy:

GET THE BOOK » *jonathanstark.com/pyfree*

TABLE OF CONTENTS

Acknowledgments 11

Introduction 13

How to respond to
"What's your hourly rate?" 14

How to respond to
"How do you price your work?" 17

How To Conduct A Sales Interview,
Part 1: The Brain Dump 19

How To Conduct A Sales Interview,
Part 2: The Why Conversation 22

How to respond to
"Can you give me a ballpark?" 26

How to respond to
"Do you guarantee your work?" 28

How to respond to
"Have you done work like this before?" 31

Nine types of discount requests 33

Just Say No 38

How to respond to "How Hard Can It Be?"
discount requests 39

How to respond to
"We're Broke" discount requests 43

How to respond to
"Sharpen Your Pencils" discount requests 46

Breakdown of my "business case" line 48

How to respond to
"Peace, Love, and Happiness"
discount requests 52

How to respond to
"Pay Your Dues" discount requests 55

How to respond to
"You're The Most Expensive"
discount requests 57

How to respond to
"How About We Treat You Like An Employee?"
discount requests 60

How to respond to
"We'll Never Get This Through Accounting"
discount requests 63

How to respond to
"It's Not Up To Us" discount requests 66

How to ask for 100% payment up-front 69

How to push back on deadlines 73

Not all deadlines are bad 77

Next Steps 79

Appendix I: More Info 81

ACKNOWLEDGMENTS

Thank you so much to the following amazing people who have helped me crystallize the thoughts contained in this book:

Alan Weiss, Anthony English, Antonis Christofides, Blair Enns, Bob Spryn, Brad Irby, Brennan Dunn, Charles Max Wood, Chris Booth, Chris Ferdinandi, Chris Moyer, Dave Sullivan, David Trejo, Don Levan, Ed Gandia, Ed Kless, Elliot Betancourt, Eric Davis, Fei Wang, Geneve Hoffman, Greg Lane, Greg Navis, Jack Templin, Jane Portman, Jason Kemp, Jean Tunis, Jeff Scornavacca, Jeff Ward, Jeremy Green, Jon Hainstock, Jorge Colon, Joshua Nussbaum, Julie Elster, Kai Davis, Katherine Porfilio, Kelli Shaver, Kelsey Kreiling, Kirk Bowman, Kurt Elster, Mandy Moore, Marcus Blankenship, Marcus Lillington, Mark Richman, Matt Inglot, Matt Krause, Matt Navarre, Michael Steele, Mojca Marš, Molly Thorsen Connelly, Nick Disabato, Paul Boag, Paul Jarvis, Philip Morgan, Reuven Lerner, Roderic Campbell, Ron Baker, Sarah Greesonbach, Seth Godin, Tomislav Car, Travis Northcutt, and Zack Gilbert.

Extra special shout outs to #PCR Mafia for being my trusted advisors, to my coaching students who have taught me more than I could ever teach them, and to all the wonderful folks on my mailing list who write me daily with ideas, encouragement, and most importantly, excellent questions.

Yours,
—J

INTRODUCTION

You can pretty much bet that any new prospect will ask one or more of the following questions early in the sales process:

- What's your hourly rate?
- Can you give me a ballpark price?
- Could you have this done by [DATE]?
- Can we get a discount?
- When can you start?

Since you know these questions are coming, why not have your answers down pat... practiced and memorized?

Clearly articulating your replies will demonstrate confidence and build trust.

Bonus points for using the opportunity to demonstrate your deep expertise by answering with unexpected but thoughtful replies.

Learn your lines, folks! It's easy and powerful.

HOW TO RESPOND TO "WHAT'S YOUR HOURLY RATE?"

When a prospective client asks:

"What's your hourly rate?"

You politely reply:

"I don't have one."

That's it. Full stop.

Exactly these four words. No variation.

Simple, clear, concise.

Try saying it out loud.

Seriously, say it out loud right now:

"I don't have one."

Easy, right? The thing is, this answer is simple (conceptually) but hard (in practice). You have to prepare it.

If you don't, you'll waffle, or stammer, or try to explain, or otherwise make excuses. *These types of responses destroy trust.*

Here are some examples of what NOT to say:

- "I don't really have one."
- "I don't actually have one."
- "I don't usually bill by the hour."
- "I prefer not to bill hourly."
- "I only charge hourly for emergency work."
- "I only charge hourly for maintenance work."
- "I used to charge $100/hr, but I don't anymore."
- "It depends on the situation."
- "I do value billing."
- "That's a stupid question."
- "Hourly billing is nuts."

Here's the thing...

When a prospect asks you, "What's your hourly rate?" it is very early in the relationship. Things are fragile and tentative. They are just trying to get to know you a little bit. They are highly tuned to even the smallest signals.

They don't want to hear you stumble on such a simple question, or soapbox about pricing theory, or dive into your entire business backstory.

Simply replying, "I don't have one," immediately sets you apart from the crowd. Upon hearing your answer, your prospect will pause to absorb what you said. There will be a short silence.

DO NOT RUSH TO FILL THIS SILENCE!

Let. It. Hang.

Even if It feels like a yawning chasm opening up before you, keep your trap shut.

The client will then ask:

"How do you price your work?"

Success! They didn't hang up on you, or scream at you, or burn you with fire. Do you know what did happen? You demonstrated confidence, you built a little trust, you pushed back on their request, and now you are having a conversation on your terms, not theirs.

HOW TO RESPOND TO "HOW DO YOU PRICE YOUR WORK?"

When a prospect asks for your hourly rate, and you tell them that you don't have one, they'll usually follow up by asking:

"How do you price your work?"

In this chapter, I'll tell you what to say and break it down into its component parts.

YOUR LINES

Here's what you say:

"I'll give you a fixed price for the entire project. That way, you'll know, prior to making a purchasing decision, exactly how much it's going to cost you. Is that acceptable?"

This answer is a bit nuanced, so let's break it down line by line:

Line 1:
"I'll give you a fixed price for the entire project."

I recommend that you deliver the first sentence verbatim. Just memorize it and practice out loud.

Line 2:
"That way, you'll know prior to making a purchasing decision exactly how much it's going cost you."

You can modify the second sentence to suit your personality and speaking style. Just make sure that it's clear that your price will be a *fixed quote, not an estimate*. This will make working with you feel less risky than working with competitors who present only estimates.

Line 3:
"Is that acceptable?"

A small percentage of organizations have rigid procurement policies that require vendors to provide hourly rates. In the unlikely event that the prospect says, "No, a project price is not acceptable," then you should say something like:

"Ah, I see. That's unfortunate. Well... I guess we're not going to be a good fit. Thank you for your time."

What?! Throw away the lead? Yes, chuck 'em.

Don't worry. You're probably not missing out on much of an opportunity. In a situation like this, the odds are good that the person you're talking to is not the real buyer; actual buyers know how to work around rigid policies when the need arises.

HOW TO CONDUCT A SALES INTERVIEW, PART 1: THE BRAIN DUMP

Once you have successfully responded to "What's your hourly rate?" and "How do you price your work?" you'll likely end up scheduling a meeting with the potential client.

In this initial sales interview, your first question should be something similar to:

"Can you tell me a little bit about the project?"

It's a big, open-ended question intended to trigger a complete brain dump. The dumping can take some time. At least 15 minutes, but probably more like 30.

But here's the thing:

Almost nothing they say will be of much value.

While they are talking, you should:

> - Listen patiently and attentively
> - Jot down any key points, interesting terms, unusual language, etc
> - Ask if you don't understand a concept, an acronym, or some industry jargon

NOTE: You should *barely talk at all* during this brain dump. You want it to end as soon as possible, but not before they've gotten everything off of their chest. You want the client to feel like they have exhausted their knowledge of the planned project.

Do not ask questions about scope, or features, or color palettes, or unit testing, or etc etc etc. These things don't matter yet. Even if you did ask, their answers would probably turn out to be wrong anyway.

Do not get excited by some novel problem that the client describes. Do not start exploring possible solutions or try to demonstrate how smart you are by describing a possible solution.

Chatting about project minutiae like scope, features, and deliverables will prolong the conversation without learning anything useful. It's just noise at this point.

The purpose of this meeting is NOT to determine scope, or identify obstacles, or agree on deliverables.

The purpose of this meeting is to *find out why the client wants someone like you to do a project like this at this point in time.*

Without the answer to this question, you have no way of knowing whether you could deliver a positive return on investment.

Without the answer to this question, you have no basis for calculating a price that would be profitable to both parties.

And if you eventually take on the project without the answer to this question, you'd be like a doctor performing heart surgery simply because the patient asked for it. (e.g., Patient: "Hey doc, I heard you do triple bypasses! Can I get me one of those?" Doctor: "Sure! Hop up on the table, and I'll grab my scalpel!")

Okay... once the brain dump is complete, what should you say next? That's where The Why Conversation comes in.

HOW TO CONDUCT A SALES INTERVIEW, PART 2: THE WHY CONVERSATION

At some point in your initial sales interview with a prospective client, they will brain dump about the proposed project for a while.

There is usually very little helpful information in this monologue, but you have to let them get it off their chest before you can get down to the heart of the matter, which is this:

Why they want to do the project at all.

Questioning the project's premise before they do the dump will frustrate or confuse them. They will gloss over the answer so they can jump to the dump.

So... you have to let them get it out of their system. Keep your mouth shut and let them vent. When they finally come up for air, you say:

"Thanks for that. Lots of helpful information here. Can we back up for a sec?"

They'll say, *"Sure!"*

And then you ask some variation of the following:

"Why is this project becoming a priority now? Has something changed?"

Typically, they'll have shared something in the dump that you can use to make this question more specific, like:

> *"You mentioned that your cart abandon-ment rate has been over 80% for 18 months. Why is it becoming a priority now?"*
>
> *"You mentioned that your main competitor just launched this new feature yesterday. Why not wait a month to see if it's adopted by the market before rushing to copy it?"*
>
> *"You mentioned that you're not 100% sure what caused the drop off in traffic. Would it make sense to take a few months to re-search the issue before proceeding with this project?"*

Once you've started asking these sorts of "Why" questions, you keep doing it...

> *"Why do this now? Wouldn't it be better to keep an eye on the issue for a few months?"*
>
> *"Why hire someone like me? Couldn't you save a ton of money by outsourcing this to a company in an emerging market?"*
>
> *"Why not use something off-the-shelf? Wouldn't that be cheaper than paying for custom code?"*
>
> *etc etc etc.*

Don't stop asking Why questions until you are convinced that you are - or are not - a good fit for the project.

THE WHY CONVERSATION

For obvious reasons, I refer to this as "The Why Conversation." Having The Why Conversation sort of feels like trying to talk the prospect out of hiring you because... well, you kind of *are* trying to talk the prospect out of hiring you.

If you CAN talk them out of hiring you, then they didn't need you that badly (i.e., the perceived value of your engagement was low, which means you couldn't have charged much).

If you CAN NOT talk them out of hiring you, then as they answer each Why question, one by one, they'll be convincing *themselves* that you are the best option.

If you conduct The Why Conversation successfully, you'll have something to base a value price on because you'll have learned:

▸ Why the project is urgent to the client
▸ What they think will happen if they don't do the project
▸ The feared business impact of failing to act now
▸ Why they think you're a good fit for the project
▸ Why they don't want to do with a cheaper option

Once you have this info, you can start to wrap the meeting up. At this point, it's pretty standard for the prospect to ask:

"Can you give me a ballpark on what this might cost?"

How should you respond to this?

Let's tackle that next...

HOW TO RESPOND TO "CAN YOU GIVE ME A BALLPARK?"

Early in the sales process, it's common for a prospective client to ask:

"Can you give me a ballpark on what this might cost?"

To which I reply (with a big smile on my face):

"Between five thousand and five hundred thousand."

This usually gets a laugh, which is what I'm going for.

(I deliver this line with a smile on my face, even if I'm on the phone... people can hear you smiling.)

You should adjust the numbers up or down into a realistic range for your services, but the high number has to be WAAAAAY higher than the lower one (e.g., like, 100 times higher).

Once the chuckling is over, I say:

"I need to crunch some numbers. Can you give me a few days to put a proposal together?"

They'll say, "Yes."

And then I say:

"Thanks. I see a few ways to tackle this project. In my proposal, I'll provide a range of options for you to choose from. I can have it to you on Monday. Will that work?"

Again, they'll say, "Yes."

And that's all there is to handling the ballpark question.

HOW TO RESPOND TO "DO YOU GUARANTEE YOUR WORK?"

If a prospect comes straight out and asks if you guarantee your work or offer refunds, it probably means that they don't wholeheartedly believe you can deliver the desired results.

This is a sign that you need to add more "street cred" (aka social proof) to your marketing and do a better job uncovering value in your initial sales interviews with The Why Conversation.

That said, you do need to decide if and how you will offer guarantees in order to prepare for questions like:

"Will you refund our money if we are not happy with your work?"

How and when to offer guarantees for the kinds of work that service providers (e.g., software developers, web designers, wedding photographers, ghostwriters, etc) typically do is a touchy subject. I offer different sorts of guarantees for different sorts of services.

For example:

- **Custom projects** - Case by case, but usually, my guarantee is along the lines of "I'll keep working until we've reached the stated goals" rather than "I'll refund your money." *(This only works if you give a fixed price for the project, of course.)*
- **Advisory retainers** - I offer a full refund at any time during the first month to make sure we're a good fit—no refunds after that.
- **Private speaking gigs** - I do not offer refunds, even if the client cancels prior to the event. They are allowed to reschedule at no charge, however.
- **Online training classes** - No refunds, but students can retake them for free.

For relatively fixed scope dev work (e.g., a productized service) that I can finish quickly, I'd offer a 100% money-back guarantee on my sales page.

(I'd also price the service accordingly, but that's another story.)

So, for a short engagement that takes maybe a half day or less (e.g., SQL performance tuning, a boudoir photo shoot, a SaaS onboarding analysis), I'd offer a 100% money-back guarantee if they were unsatisfied with the outcome.

This type of service is analogous to bringing my car to a mechanic to have it tuned up. If the car is still running rough when I leave, I'd expect them to either redo the work or refund my money.

WAIT... GIVE THEIR MONEY BACK?

When discussing guarantees with my students, they sometimes ask:

"Have you ever had to actually refund money?"

In ten years of business, I think I've only given four refunds, all of which were voluntary (i.e., the client didn't ask for them):

- $10,000 refunded for an iPad web app project (I returned their check immediately after the kickoff meeting because it was clear that the CEO was going to sabotage the project)
- $5,000 refunded for an iPad app that I couldn't get working properly (my fault for choosing a lousy tool)
- $5,000 refunded for work on an iPad app prototype that went off the rails (my fault for not controlling scope creep)
- $600 refunded for delivering a roadmap a few weeks late (my fault for letting myself get overbooked)

If we throw out the first one (since I hadn't done any work yet), refunds amount to a fraction of a percentage point of my revenue over the same period (i.e., they haven't been a big deal for me at all).

HOW TO RESPOND TO "HAVE YOU DONE WORK LIKE THIS BEFORE?"

What should you say when a prospective client asks:

"Have you done work like this before?"

This is a pointed question. It is meant to disqualify you. But if you're ready for it, you can use it to your advantage.

Here's an example from my mobile strategy consulting days:

I was contacted by an organization in the credit union space that was looking for some expert advice about mobile UX for banking applications. At a critical point in the sales cycle, I was asked, "Have you done work like this before?"

Since I knew that this prospect was familiar with my expertise in mobile, I understood that the real question was:

"Have you done any mobile work *for credit unions*?"

The truth was that I had never worked with a credit union before. I had never even had an account at a credit union. To my knowledge, this was literally the very first time I had ever spoken to a "credit union person" of any kind.

So here's what I said:

"I have zero experience with credit unions, which is exactly why you need me. I'm a complete outsider. You're looking for unbiased feedback and recommendations on your mobile initiative from the standpoint of the typical end user. Someone who understands the jargon and inner workings of a credit union could never deliver what you need."

This type of "fresh eyes" approach won't work in every case, but it works in many of them. As an added benefit, it serves to disarm your competitors who DO have experience in the vertical. They'll pitch their experience as a strength, but it will be viewed by the prospect as a weakness.

(BTW - I landed the gig, which ended up bringing in over $50k in revenue. I don't track my hours, but I spent about 30-40 hours on it, which amounts to an effective hourly rate of around $1300/hr. Even if I'm horribly wrong and it was more like 80 hours, my effective hourly rate was still north of $600/hr. And yes, the client was delighted with the outcome and ended up referring me to four other organizations in the credit union space.)

NINE TYPES OF DISCOUNT REQUESTS

Following are nine types of discounts that I have encountered over the years.

I'll cover each individually in subsequent chapters, but here's the overall list with descriptions and some real-world examples:

1. HOW HARD COULD IT BE?

The client views you as a laborer (or themselves as an expert) and has a hopelessly naive idea of what the work entails.

"It seems all you really need to do is just X. Can you help me understand why you think it's going to cost that much? I mean, I trust you 100%, but it seems like $5,000 would be plenty to just X."

2. WE'RE BROKE

The client claims that they simply don't have the budget to cover your fee. This could be true, a misconception, or a bluff.

"It's hard enough for us to make money as it is. Could you do it for $XXX?"

3. SHARPEN YOUR PENCILS

Client vaguely implies that you need to lower your price, but without directly asking for a discount.

Example from a reader:

Right there in the meeting, I estimated $400 USD for the work at my usual rate of $20/hr. The response from the client was something like: "Ok... I guess you'll be sharpening your pencil for us" (Which is a literal translation of an Argentinian expression; I'm not sure it makes much sense in English).

"I need you to sharpen your pencils. Can you do that?"

"That's higher than I expected, so let's leave it for now and revisit when we've done a few more projects together, and we know it'll be valuable."

4. PEACE, LOVE, AND HAPPINESS

The client implies that since they're a not-for-profit entity, you should be, too.

"We're a not-for-profit organization. Do you have a special rate for clients like us?"

5. PAY YOUR DUES

The client suggests implicitly or explicitly that giving them a discount now will result in some combination of more work, more notoriety, more clients, or more profits at some indeterminate point in the future.

"We are hoping to use more of your services in the new year. And we usually get a discount when we buy more of something."

"If you can lower your price, you'll have lots of work coming through from us."

Example from a reader:

"When saying an hourly rate (which I'm working on getting out of my system), I often get people asking if we'd take less if it's a bigger project."

6. YOU'RE THE MOST EXPENSIVE

The client explicitly states that they have received lower prices from other vendors.

"Your proposal is the most expensive we got, but we want to buy from you. What can you do for me?"

"Company X said they would do it for half your rate!"

7. HOW ABOUT WE TREAT YOU LIKE AN EMPLOYEE?

The client tries to entice you into some sort of employment or employment-related arrangement.

Example from a reader:

"I'm preparing for a sales call with a prospect in twenty minutes. They've already asked, 'Would you be interested in the engineering manager position?' Which happens fairly frequently: 'We like you so much, in fact, that we'd like to hire you and get all of your time for a whole lot less money.' It's the ultimate discount ask."

Example from a reader:

"The one I get most often is from startups who ask if I will do the work in exchange for equity or for part equity/part cash."

"Can we pay you with equity?"

8. WE'LL NEVER GET THIS THROUGH ACCOUNTING

The client cites some company policy, cultural attitude, or financial threshold that will cause the project fee or hourly rate to be rejected out of hand.

"This price seems fair to me, but I'll never get the CFO to approve it."

9. IT'S NOT UP TO US

The client is reselling your services to another party and wittingly or unwittingly uses your lack of direct contact with the real buyer to their advantage.

"The client will never agree to this rate."

Example from a reader:

"I was working through agents, and they said, 'The client wouldn't have the budget for that.' In one case, the agent said: 'The client is going to translate that roadmapping session as a very high daily rate.'"

JUST SAY NO

Over the following several chapters, I'm going to get into some pretty nuanced answers to variations of the question:

"Can we get a discount?"

Before I do that, I want to make sure that one thing is perfectly clear...

The answer is:

"No."

Of course, you shouldn't bluntly respond with a no. And in different situations, there may even be an exception.

But just so you know... if you get overwhelmed by all of the tactics that are to follow, a polite "No" is almost always better than a "Yes."

HOW TO RESPOND TO "HOW HARD CAN IT BE?" DISCOUNT REQUESTS

Let's assume you've given a client a fixed price quote for $5,000 to do X, and the client responds with something like this:

"Can you help me understand why you think it's going to cost that much? I mean, I trust you 100%, but it seems $5000 would be plenty just to do X."

I lump this sort of request into the following category:

How Hard Could It Be? - i.e., the client views you as a laborer (or themselves as an expert) and has a hopelessly naive idea of what the work entails.

There are a number of ways you might reply to this depending on your history with the client, their level of technical proficiency, the complexity of the work, how much you think they really trust you, and so on.

Therefore, the following list wouldn't all work in every situation, but at least one should work in any given situation.

YOUR LINES

Without further ado, here are your lines:

Line #1:

"$5000 would be plenty just to do X if that was all there was to it, but there are always surprises with work like this. As an expert, I feel it's my responsibility to shoulder the risk of the unknown on your behalf. The alternative would be to low-ball price now and then come back for more money later because of some 'surprise.' All projects have surprises, so I consider the low-ball approach to be negligent."

Why it works:

You are pointing out that projects are risky and that you are the one taking the risk. To drill the point home, you paint a picture of the alternative, which is them getting nickel and dimed by inexperienced or unscrupulous competitors.

Line #2

"X is just the surface-level manifestation of the work. There are several things that need to be done under the hood to make X work. For example, [FAIRLY DETAILED EXPLANATION OF COMPLEX NUANCE]"

Why it works:

You are telling them that it's more complicated than they think and then giving them a quick look behind the scenes. This works on dabblers (i.e., the self-proclaimed "I know enough to be dangerous" type of client) because they enjoy the behind-the-scenes stuff but are easily overwhelmed by it. I'm generally against "educating the client," but this is one case where it can be effective.

Line #3

"X is the focus, but there are quite a few unknowns that could be significant. If you'd like, we can start with a diagnostic phase to uncover any surprises. I could do that for [NON-TRIVIAL FRACTION OF ORIGINAL PRICE], and it would take about [NON-TRIVIAL AMOUNT OF TIME]. After we have more information, I'll re-quote X. This approach often reduces the price, but I can't guarantee it. The price for X could even go up."

Why it works:

You give them an option that feels less risky because it is less rushed and more deliberative. Even if it ends up costing the same or more over time, this can work with risk-averse or decision-averse clients. If it turns out that you can offer X for less than your initially quoted price, it's not really a discount. Instead, you have changed the definition of X and priced it accordingly.

Line #4

"I'm curious... When you say '$5000 should be plenty for X', what are you basing your calculation on?"

Why it works:

You are turning the "how did you come up with your numbers" question around. This will force them to admit that their suggested price is irrational because it is based on gut instinct, something a friend told them, unrelated past work with you or another vendor, etc. This reversal needs to be delivered delicately. If you don't convey a genuine sense of curiosity, it will likely come across as defensive or combative.

HOW TO RESPOND TO "WE'RE BROKE" DISCOUNT REQUESTS

Let's assume you've provided a quote, and your contact responds with something like this:

"It's hard enough for us to make money as it is. Could you do it for $X instead?"

This request falls into the following category:

We're Broke - The client claims that they simply don't have the budget to cover your fee. This could be true, a misconception, or a bluff.

Let's imagine that you have some reason to believe that you know which of the three possibilities is the case:

1. They really don't have the money
2. They think they don't have the money
3. They're bluffing

YOUR LINES

I've broken your lines down into sections based on what you think the client's situation is.

1. They really don't have the money

If you really believe that the client doesn't have the money, your qualification process needs to be improved. In your sales and marketing materials, you must express - implicitly or explicitly - that you are expensive. You shouldn't be wasting time on clients like this.

Okay, but here we are, and you have to reply...

If you DON'T want the gig, say:

"I can't do it for less, but I'd be happy to recommend a junior colleague who might be able to work within that budget. Would you like me to make an introduction?"

If you DO want the gig, say:

"I can't do the work as described for less, but I'd be willing to work with you to try to create an option that will meet your budget."

NOTE: I specifically address non-profits in a later chapter.

2. They think they don't have the money

The client says they don't have the money, but you have reason to believe that they do have it somewhere. In this case, it's a priority issue, not a resource issue.

Here's what you say:

"C'mon... You guys are probably spending more to have the trash cans emptied. What's the real objection here?"

NOTE 1: This is a tricky one that is best delivered with humor in person or over the phone.

NOTE 2: To avoid this in the future, do a better job uncovering the client's perceived value with The Why Conversation during your initial sales interview.

3. They're bluffing

If you believe that the client has the money allocated and is just in the habit of asking for a discount regardless of the situation, here's what you say:

"Thanks for asking, but I just can't make a business case for lowering my price. PLMK if you're willing to move forward at the quoted amount. If I haven't heard back by this time next week, I'll assume you've gone in another direction."

WHAT IF YOU DON'T KNOW?

If you don't know for sure which of the three scenarios above is the actual client situation, default to number three (i.e., "...can't make a business case...")

HOW TO RESPOND TO "SHARPEN YOUR PENCILS" DISCOUNT REQUESTS

Let's assume you've provided a quote, and your contact responds with a variation on one of the following:

"Ok... I guess you'll be sharpening your pencil for us."

"I need you to sharpen your pencils. Can you do that?"

"That's higher than I expected, so let's leave it for now and revisit when we've done a few more projects together, and we know it'll be valuable."

I'd never even heard the "sharpen your pencils" euphemism before, but apparently, it's not uncommon outside the US. It's such a perfect example of this type of request that I named the category after it.

Sharpen Your Pencils - The client vaguely implies that you need to lower your price, but without directly asking for a discount.

YOUR LINES

In a case like this, you're probably dealing with someone who routinely asks for discounts because they have learned that the vast majority of sellers will immediately grant one for no good reason.

Assuming that you have worked with the client to come to an agreement about the perceived value of the outcome, this behavior borders on insulting.

Historically, I have dealt with this in one of two ways:

1. **Go Dark** - I simply do not respond to the request. This sort of client behavior is a major red flag. If I'm busy enough, I won't even dignify it with a response. If they spontaneously backpedal, I will rethink the red flag. Otherwise, they're forgotten.
2. **Sorry, no!** - I politely, succinctly, and clearly say "Nope!" like so:

"Thanks for asking, but I just can't make a business case for lowering my price. PLMK if you're willing to move forward at the quoted amount. If I haven't heard back by this time next week, I'll assume you've gone in another direction."

Alert readers will note that I used this line in a previous scenario. You'll likely see it again in a future scenario. It's my go-to reply when saying NO to a request for a discount. It's a good one to practice out loud and commit to memory.

Come to think of it, let's break it down...

BREAKDOWN OF MY "BUSINESS CASE" LINE

In two of the previous scenarios about how to respond to discount requests, I have suggested using the following line:

"Thanks for asking, but I just can't make a business case for lowering my price."

This is my default fallback for delivering a polite "No" without having to think too hard about it.

When I first shared this line with my mailing list, I received the following question:

Can you explain your thinking behind this phrase? It's unclear what that means, and I would worry the client would say the same.

Happy to!

BREAKDOWN

I'll break down the key fragments:

"Thanks for asking"

Translation: "I'm not annoyed that you asked for a discount."

It sets an upbeat tone for the rest of the message. I don't want to come across as defensive.

"but I just can't make"

Translation: "I spent time thinking about your request"

Even though I'm going to say no, I did give it some consideration. I don't want to come across as dismissive.

"a business case"

Translation: "You're essentially asking for a personal favor"

The client did not give a compelling business reason to justify a discount.

OVERALL TONE

In my original example, I purposely use "soft focus" words because that's the way most of my clients communicate. You could create your own variant by rewording the fragments.

For example:

"Hey there! It's totally cool that you asked for a discount. I re-crunched the numbers for you, but I still think my price is on point."

Or:

"Hi Bob, Regarding your discount request - I completely understand that this is a significant investment, and I did spend some time going back over the numbers. Still, I think the quoted price is justified given my level of involvement and the upside for your company."

Both of these communicate the same core message as my original, but with different words:

1. I'm not mad
2. I gave it some thought
3. The original price is reasonable
4. I'm sticking to it

A word of caution: if you want to compose your own variation of this line, keep it short (20-40 words max). If you respond with a long message, it comes across as defensive and needy. You don't have to make a case, justify your position, or explain your reasoning. A polite No will suffice.

POSSIBLE CLIENT RESPONSES

There are only three ways the client can respond to your polite No:

1. Yes - the client makes the purchase at the original price.
2. No - the client does not make the purchase.
3. Maybe - the client asks for more info or continues haggling.

"Yes," and "No" need no further attention from a sales perspective.

But what about that "Maybe?"

If the client wants to keep talking about the discount after you have politely declined, you're probably not going to get the gig, or if you do, you'll regret it.

If you want to salvage the sale anyway, turn the question around and make the client justify in business terms why they deserve a discount.

Something like:

Client: "We really can't move forward unless you give us that discount."

You: "Is there a specific reason for that?"

At this point, the client will most likely state some rationale that you can address with more specific lines that I've provided elsewhere (e.g., we haven't got the money, we should get a bulk discount, your price isn't the lowest, etc.).

HOW TO RESPOND TO "PEACE, LOVE, AND HAPPINESS" DISCOUNT REQUESTS

Let's say you're having an initial meeting with a prospective client, and they ask something like this:

"We're a not-for-profit organization. Do you have a special rate for clients like us?"

This request falls into the following category:

Peace, Love, and Happiness - The client implies that since they're a not-for-profit entity, you should be, too.

Typically, non-profits are mission-oriented organizations dedicated to making the world a better place rather than creating profits for shareholders.

The fact that they don't create profits does not mean that they are broke. A quick search on guidestar.org shows that 469 non-profit organizations brought in over a billion dollars of income last year. 4,485 orgs brought in over $100M.

So...

YOUR LINES

Optional Pre-Line

If you'd like to break the ice with a bit of humor, you can plaster a big smile on your face and say:

"Why yes! My rate for tax-exempt organizations is 20% higher than my standard rate ;-)"

When the uncomfortable laughter dies down, you can deliver the real line...

Non-Optional Real Line

"Actually, I don't have set rates. Every project is different, and I price each one individually. I take everything into consideration when setting my prices, including non-profit status, mission, and so on."

Of course, these lines won't work if you bill by the hour, but as you know - I think hourly billing is nuts.

AN ASIDE ABOUT MISSION-DRIVEN ORGS

I take an organization's mission into consideration with all prospective clients regardless of non-profit/for-profit status. Working with a group that is dedicated to changing the world in a way that aligns with my worldview decreases my cost, which means I can offer a lower price without sacrificing profits.

That said, I wouldn't list any explicit discount on my quote (e.g., I don't include a line item like -> "20%

non-profit discount"). Instead, I might say some-thing like, "I agree with and support your mission and have taken that into consideration favorably when setting my fees."

HOW TO RESPOND TO "PAY YOUR DUES" DISCOUNT REQUESTS

Let's assume you've provided a proposal to a prospective client, and your contact responds with a variation on one of the following:

"We are hoping to use more of your services in the new year. And we usually get a discount when we buy more of something."

"If you can lower your price, you'll have lots of work coming through from us."

"Would you lower your hourly rate if we make it a bigger project?"

These sorts of requests fall into the following category:

Pay Your Dues - The client suggests implicitly or explicitly that giving them a discount now will result in some combination of more work, more notoriety, more clients, or more profits at some indeterminate point in the future.

When a prospect makes such a request, what I hear in my head is:

"If you agree to this crappy deal now, we promise to offer you more crappy deals in the future!"

Um... no thanks.

THE STABILITY CARROT

The carrot they are dangling in front of you is stability. Giving in to this sort of request will instantly create a destructive client relationship dynamic.

You will have validated their suspicion that you need them more than they need you. That you are so desperate for work that the mere suggestion of a steady paycheck is enough to convince you to lower your price.

Bad clients don't magically turn into good clients. In fact, it's tough to convert bad clients into good ones. It's easier to attract good clients than to transform bad ones.

YOUR LINES

The default answer to any "Pay Your Dues" request is our old standby, the polite No:

"Thanks for asking, but I just can't make a business case for lowering my price. PLMK if you're willing to move forward at the quoted amount. If I haven't heard back by this time next week, I'll assume you've gone in another direction."

HOW TO RESPOND TO "YOU'RE THE MOST EXPENSIVE" DISCOUNT REQUESTS

Let's assume you've provided a quote, and your contact responds with a variation on one of the following:

> ▶ "Your proposal is the most expensive we got, but we want to buy from you. What can you do for me?"
> ▶ "Company X said they would do it for half your price!"

These sorts of requests fall into the following category:

You're The Most Expensive - The client explicitly states that they have received lower prices from other vendors.

MARKETING FAIL

If you get hit with this one, you need to up your sales and marketing game. Do a better job making it clear in your messaging that you are a premium option (i.e., the best, not the cheapest).

You can do this simply by publishing your prices on your website. If you don't want to publish your prices (or can't because you only do custom work), you can add some copy to your contact page that indicates the minimum investment that they should be willing to make.

Something like:

Custom projects start at $20,000 and can go as high as $200,000. Can you presently afford this level of investment? [YES/NO checkbox]

You can further cement your position as the premium option once you have a prospect on the phone by trying to talk them out of working with you.

For example:

- "Why not outsource this to a cheaper team overseas?"
- "Have you considered using something off the shelf?"
- "Why not do this project in-house?"

Assuming they reject all of your suggestions, they will have explained to you (and themselves) exactly why cheaper alternatives are not viable options for them.

(For more on this, see "The Why Conversation" chapter elsewhere in this book.)

YOUR LINES

Hopefully, your improved messaging will result in you never getting this sort of request again. But if you do get it, here are some lines you can use:

- "If you're looking for the cheapest option, I'm definitely not right for this project."
- "If price is the only consideration, you should definitely go with one of the other vendors."
- "I was under the impression that choosing low-cost vendors is what got you in this situation in the first place. Was I misinformed?"
- "You made it clear that this project is critical to your business. Do you really want to trust it to the lowest bidder?"

Once you deliver your line, they will most likely ask you to justify why they should pay a premium to work with you. Be prepared to differentiate yourself from the cheaper options.

HOW TO RESPOND TO "HOW ABOUT WE TREAT YOU LIKE AN EMPLOYEE?" DISCOUNT REQUESTS

When presented with a price that seems high to them, a prospect will sometimes propose the idea of paying you in equity, a percentage of profits, or just outright hiring you as an internal employee.

For example:

- ▸ "Would you be interested in the engineering manager position?"
- ▸ "We like you. So much, in fact, that we'd like to hire you full-time."
- ▸ "Can we pay you with equity?"

I lump these sorts of requests into the following category:

How About We Treat You Like An Employee? - The client tries to entice you into some sort of employment or employment-related arrangement.

YOUR LINES

I'll tackle the equity question first.

1. Can we pay you with equity?

If I wanted to take on massive amounts of risk, I'd found my own startup. The idea of betting on someone else's gamble is almost laughable. Here's what I'd say:

"I believe in what you guys are doing, but I'm pretty conservative business-wise. My risk tolerance is much lower than yours, so equity isn't a good fit for me."

The message I'm trying to send is:

"I'm sure I'll regret not taking the offer when you're acquired for billions, but I'm just not a gambler."

In other words, it's not that I think they're going to fail - it's that I'm risk averse. ("It's not you, it's me")

2. Can we hire you full-time?

After years of being my own boss, I doubt I'd last two weeks in a traditional job. Plus, I'd have to spin down a bunch of client, student, and partner relationships. It would take too much time, even if I wanted to do it. There's just no feasible salary that could make me take on a 9-5, so it's not even worth discussing the details with them. Here's what I'd say:

"Wow, I'm flattered by the offer! Unfortunately, I'm just not at a place in my life where I'd be prepared to make such an enormous change."

Like the previous line, this one takes the stance of "it's not you, it's me" - i.e., "You guys have an amazing company, and I'd be proud to call myself an employee, but I'm set in my ways, and it's too big a change for me."

HOW TO RESPOND TO "WE'LL NEVER GET THIS THROUGH ACCOUNTING" DISCOUNT REQUESTS

At some point in the sales process, your prospect may say something like:

- *"Company policy requires that we pay contractors by the hour."*
- *"The maximum I can pay out without approval of senior management is $5000."*
- *"Our systems don't support pre-payment for services."*

I categorize these sorts of statements like so:

We'll Never Get This Through Accounting - The client cites some company policy, cultural attitude, or financial threshold that will cause the project fee or hourly rate to be rejected out of hand.

These sorts of objections are not specifically discount requests, but they do attempt to force you into unfavorable payment terms. It could be that the contact truly feels hamstrung by rigid policies, or it could be that they are bluffing.

YOUR LINES

My approach in situations like these is to play hard-ball - politely, of course. Rather than throw up my hands and accept the broken policy, I approach the restriction as a hurdle that my contact and I need to overcome together.

For example...

Contact: *"The maximum I can pay out without approval of senior management is $5000."*

Me: *"Understood. Well, I know how important this engagement is to your company. Is there some way we could work around this?"*

Contact: *"For instance?"*

Me: *"What if we broke the project into 3 phases, each priced at $5000?"*

Contact: *"That works for me."*

Or...

Contact: *"Company policy requires that we pay contractors by the hour."*

Me: *"Hm... is there a maximum hourly rate?"*

Contact: *"I don't think so."*

Me: *"How about I invoice for 1 hour at $3,500?"*

Contact: *"Might work. I'll try it."*

Or...

Contact: "Our systems don't support pre-payment for services."

Me: "How about I send you a net-30 invoice today, and we set the project start date for a month from today?"

Contact: "That's fine. Yeah, we can't get started for two weeks anyway."

If we can't come up with a solution and my only option is to "take it or leave it," I walk away.

True buyers can work around rigid policies. If you're not talking to the true buyer, you're not going to have much luck overcoming these sorts of objections.

HOW TO RESPOND TO "IT'S NOT UP TO US" DISCOUNT REQUESTS

Let's say you're approached by an agency that needs you to give them a quote for some portion of a project for one of their clients.

You submit a proposal, and they reply with one of the following:

"We are handling the client, so we'd like you to give us a wholesale rate."

"The client wouldn't have the budget for that."

"The client is going to translate that roadmapping session as a very high daily rate."

I group these into this category:

It's Not Up To Us - The client is reselling your services to another party and wittingly or unwittingly uses your lack of direct contact with the real buyer to their advantage.

YOUR LINES

Other than a polite refusal to decrease your rates, there's not much you can say in this scenario. Value is in the buyer's mind, so the only way to establish it - and therefore justify your fees - is to talk to the client directly.

Working through an agency can be a good way to shore up cash flow in a slow period, but it's not a good way to build a business long-term. If you have to do it at all, view it as a stopgap measure while you attract your own clients directly.

WHOLESALE?

Okay, so you can just use my "polite no" line discussed in previous sections when you find yourself in this scenario, but I wanted to comment specifically on the "wholesale rate" argument above. It's just so ridiculous I couldn't help myself.

A wholesale discount is based primarily on high-quantity sales, not the fact that the middleman is dealing with the customer. If the middleman is not buying from you in volume and paying 100% in advance, a wholesale rate doesn't apply. They're not retailing your services. They're outsourcing to you. It's not the same thing.

Furthermore, in a professional services business, the client relationship is the most valuable asset. Claiming that you should agree to a lower fee because you don't own the client relationship is backward. You should charge MORE because you don't own the client relationship.

Here's what you could say:

"So if I agree to handle the client, my proposed rate is acceptable?"

"So, you're saying you'd like to pay in advance for a bulk purchase of my services? If I'm not mistaken, that's the basis for a wholesale price."

"Not handling the client is a liability for me. It makes my job harder. Come to think of it, I should probably raise my price... but if you want to move forward now, I'll honor the quote."

HOW TO ASK FOR 100% PAYMENT UP-FRONT

Perhaps the most shocking element of my project proposal template is that I routinely ask for 100% payment up-front.

Over the years, I've gotten a bunch of questions from readers about this unorthodox stipulation. Here are the three most common:

- Why I ask for 100% up-front payment
- How often I "get away with it"
- What I do when clients push back

I'm going to answer all of those questions here, but before I do, you need to know something very important:

I NEVER lower my prices once I have submitted a proposal.

Seriously. Never, ever.

Since I refuse to budge on price, I need to give myself room to negotiate in other areas. This is where my payment terms come in.

In case you haven't read through my proposal template yet, here's a typical example of the payment terms I offer:

TERMS AND CONDITIONS

I never assess an hourly or daily fee since you should not have to make an investment decision every time my assistance may be needed. This is a unique feature of my consulting practice.

The pricing for each option is as follows: option 1 is $5,000.00, option 2 is $12,000.00, and option 3 is $25,000.00 USD. Please note that these are fixed prices, not estimates. You will not pay a dime more than your selected price. The fee must be paid in full on acceptance to schedule the project. I am available to start on Monday, January 6, 2024. This quote is good for 14 days.

Roughly 80% of the time, clients agree to these payment terms without question. In the 20% of cases where a client doesn't, their reply is usually one of the following:

1. "Are you CRAZY?!" (aka Sticker Shock)
2. "How about 50% now and 50% on completion?" (aka 50/50 Terms)

YOUR LINES

Sticker Shock

In the "Are you CRAZY?!" scenario, I misjudged the value to the buyer, and my prices were just way too high. The prospect is suffering from an acute case of sticker shock. It's almost impossible to revive the deal at this point, so I usually just thank them for their time and move on.

50/50 Terms

In the "How about 50% now and 50% on comple-tion?" scenario, my prices are in the ballpark, but I haven't built up quite enough trust with the client. To mitigate their perceived risk, the client offers 50/50 payment terms - i.e., "How about we do 50% up-front, 50% when the work is done?"

My reply to them looks like this:

We can discuss, but I don't think it is in your best interest. A custom project is like a lake freezing - at some point, you are sure it's solid, but you never know exactly when it happened :-)

In other words, we are not going to know exactly when this project is done. Tying the final payment to the delivery date will put pressure on you to sign off too soon.

If some bug crops up in a weird corner case three months after your sign-off, I'd prefer to just fix it for free under the terms of this agreement (vs. what most other consultants would do: "Sorry, you signed off. I'll fix it, but it's going to cost you.")

To remove the sign-off issue, what would you think about doing 50% to get started and 50% in 30 days?

Almost every prospect to whom I've suggested this alternative has accepted. Once or twice, I've had a prospect balk at my suggested date (i.e., 30 days from project start), to which I say:

That's fine. The exact date doesn't matter to me. Pick whatever date you think is reasonable, and we can get started.

In this case, the client will probably pick a date around when they think the project will be completed. This date will almost surely be too early, but having agreed to a specific fixed date for the final payment allows everyone to relax about the sign-off (because there won't be a sign-off).

A wonderful side effect of this agreement is that if the client goes dark, you won't really care because it doesn't delay your final payment. They can take all the time in the world to respond to requests for feedback, provide copy changes, send FTP info, etc...

It won't matter to you because you'll still get paid in full on a known schedule and can do other work while you wait for them to get back to you—no pressure for you, no pressure for them.

WIN WIN

Ultimately, asking for 100% up-front is better for you, better for the client, and better for the project. Give it a shot on your next proposal - you'll be pleasantly surprised by the results.

HOW TO PUSH BACK ON DEADLINES

What should you say during the sales process when a client asks:

"Can you have this project done by [DATE]?"

This is a common question in the sales process. And it's understandable why a prospect would want to know when you'd be done. But that doesn't change the fact that blurting out a date would be a very risky thing to do.

You need to push back, but how do you do so in a way that is not combative or off-putting?

You **don't** want to say things like:

- ▸ "Sorry, I don't agree to project deadlines."
- ▸ "If you think anyone can control the deadline on a big project like this, you're delusional."
- ▸ "Stark says arbitrary project deadlines are bad!"

YOUR LINES

Instead, **explain to the client why setting a deadline would be bad** *for them*:

- ▸ "A deadline will put pressure on both of us to sign off before we're really done. This will almost certainly lead to maintenance charges after delivery."
- ▸ "A deadline like this will create the illusion of certainty. This would be a very bad thing if you're planning to schedule other things based on that date."
- ▸ "There are many unknowns at this stage, but I'd be happy to draft a timeline with the known dependencies. This will be a living document that we can review and update on our weekly calls. The timeline will give you visibility into and some control over the process. It will likely expand quickly in the early stages, but over time, the velocity of change will decrease, and a realistic delivery date will start to come into focus."

While you're at it, you could consider mentioning that anyone who promises to meet their arbitrary deadline is probably doing so out of inexperience or opportunism.

What do I mean by that? I'll explain by way of analogy.

IMAGINE THAT YOU'RE A WEDDING PLANNER

Imagine that you're a wedding planner. You receive an email from a bride about helping her plan her wedding. You jump on a phone call with her. You speak for 30 minutes, and she is perfectly delightful.

But then...

The bride says that she wants you to guarantee that it will be sunny on her wedding day.

You are taken aback for a second but politely explain that you are not in control of the weather and that you are very sorry, but you just can't guarantee that it will be sunny on her wedding day.

In response, she explains all the reasons that she would like it to be sunny on her wedding day and what a catastrophe it would be if it rained, and couldn't you just make an exception in her case?

Her request is insane, but still, you experience internal turmoil. It's perfectly reasonable for this bride to *want* a sunny wedding day, and you genuinely *would love* to be able to guarantee such a thing.

But it's impossible!!!

SO WHAT DO YOU DO?

Would you risk it and say, "Sure, I'll guarantee a sunny day," to get the gig and then hope like hell that it turns out that way? Of course not. That would be certifiably bonkers and borderline unethical.

Or would you be honest and say:

"I dearly wish I could control the weather, but I can't; in fact, no one can. But I understand your concern and would be happy to provide contingency plans for every possibility, be it wind, rain, tornado, or sandstorm. Would that be acceptable?"

Presumably, you'd opt for the honest "No one can control the weather" answer.

So why would you answer differently when a potential client asks you to commit to a deadline for a big, complex project?

Any project of the slightest significance is a collaboration between at least a dozen (or more!) people. You – as an outside consultant – have no more control over the responsiveness of the participants than you do over the weather.

Not even the client's CEO can guarantee an on-time delivery for the project!

There are simply too many variables. Nobody has even a modicum of control over all of them.

Committing to a deadline on a complex project is like guaranteeing a sunny wedding day - it's understandable why the client would want such a thing, but it's an absurd request and should be politely rejected as such.

Just like the wedding example, one thing you *can* do instead of agreeing to a project deadline is to offer contingency plans if the desired outcome is in jeopardy.

NOT ALL DEADLINES ARE BAD

One last thought on deadlines...

I'm sometimes asked:

"Are all deadlines bad?"

No, some deadlines are fine.

My stance on never agreeing to deadlines is specifically with regard to **complex projects**. My reasoning is that no one can control the deadline because it's an ongoing collaboration, often between quite a few people.

For example...

Client: "I know we haven't even started [big project with many stakeholders] yet, but when will it be done?"

Me: "It's impossible to know exactly when we'll be done. If everything goes perfectly, it'll take at least [X months] to complete. But nothing ever goes perfectly."

That said, there are other kinds of deadlines that I'm not necessarily against.

For example, some folks asked about having sprint "deadlines" every other week.

Lumping a list of tasks into a two-week sprint is fine because the work is broken down in a very granular way. The number of people involved in each task is often just one or two. This drastically decreases the potential number of interactions, which increases the chances of the estimates being accurate.

So, not all deadlines are bad.

NEXT STEPS

Okay, let's recap...

In this short book, you have learned at least twenty ways to specifically respond to questions that your prospective clients will almost surely ask you at some point in the future.

So... There's no excuse for being unprepared!

Learn. Your. Lines.

Practice them out loud, commit them to memory, add them to your text expander software, keep them in a swipe file on your desktop, print them out, and post them on your wall.

I don't care how you do it but do *something* so that the next time a client puts you on the spot, you know exactly how to respond quickly, clearly, and with confidence.

Thank you for reading. I wish you the best of luck in your business and hope you'll let me know how it goes. You can always email me with questions, comments, cheers, jeers, or typos at jstark@jonathanstark.com

I look forward to hearing from you!

Yours,
—J

APPENDIX I: MORE INFO

If you're looking for more info, I maintain a page of free resources that you can find at https://jonathanstark.com/free

DAILY LIST ARCHIVE

I've been sending messages to my email list every day since the summer of 2016. You can peruse the back catalog at http://jonathanstark.com/archive

QUESTIONS?

Any questions? Shoot me an email at jstark@jonathanstark.com, and I'll get back to you as soon as I can. Pro tip: the shorter your email is, the faster I'll be able to get back to you.

YOUR FREE BOOK IS WAITING

LOOKING FOR MORE?

You might enjoy a free copy of my book on how to make your business more memorable, attractive, and unique in the minds of your ideal clients.

Pigeonhole Yourself:
Transform Your Positioning From Soggy To Solid With 21 Real-World Examples.

Inside, you'll learn:

- The #1 thing you must do before engaging in marketing of any kind
- How to get word of mouth referrals without even asking
- The one thing to say when someone asks, "So... what do you do?"
- The 4 components of a laser-focused positioning statement
- The secret to differentiating yourself from your competition
- and more...

Click the button below for your free copy: